# Grannie Knows Best

## God, what does Justice look Like?

### Aria L. Suber

# YOKEDink LLC

Copyright© 2019 by Aria L. Suber

This work is previously self-published, and now pulled from the original 12 short stories of Grannie Knows Best- Breaking News Biblical Bedtime Stories written and self-published by Aria L. Suber.

All rights reserved, including the right to reproduce this book or portions thereof in any form whatsoever.

For Information contact Yokedink at yokedink.com

ISBN 978-0-9981116-3-6 (paperback)

Unless otherwise indicated, all the names, characters, businesses, places, events, and incidents in this book are either the product of the author's imagination or used in a fictitious manner. These Realistic stories are a work of fiction, and the author has taken realistic fiction situations and her imagination to express how Jesus Christ wants to be a part of any life if they will believe and open their hearts to him.

Welcome, come on in! I'm Grannie. I look forward to sharing my stories with you, and I pray that you learn and grow from each story, it's never too early or too late to learn about God. Inside these pages, you'll see God loves all of us, and how we all have good and bad days. I try my best to point others in Gods direction.

*Love,*

*Grannie*

# Grannie Knows Best

God, what does Justice look Like?

# God, what does Justice look like?
§

AS Grannie sits in the living room, she hears the voice of reporter Ro-Collins. "In Breaking News, downtown there has been" at that moment Grannie seemed to be in a daze as her mind went back to 1955 and 1957. She was between 18-20 years old. The civil rights movement was in full bloom, and everyone around her had a reason to stand for the rights of people. Grannie had the option to boycott, refuse to ride the buses and even go to Arkansas.

What weighed on Mattie the most was that one of her grandmas was white. Mattie knew she had to take a stand for something, but she didn't know which way to stand. At twenty, Grannie wasn't a Grannie; she wasn't even a mother. Her friends and family called her Mattie. Mattie and her friends all believed that a change had to come, and they could play a role in these changes. They didn't want their children to deal with the sadness and unfairness they faced every day.

Mattie stood in her grandmother's front room as she heard the words. "In Breaking News, The Little Rock Nine." Just then her grandmother entered the room and said, "Mattie, please turn off the TV," but Mattie said, "grandma,

NO Ma'am." "I must see this, and you wouldn't understand what's going on, being a white woman!" Her grandma walked towards the TV and turned it off, then said, "Mattie come and sit down next to me!" The conversation they had that day would

be the stand Mattie embraced the rest of her life.

As Grannie snapped out of her daze, she listened to Ro Collins report the shooting that had taken place downtown due to the color of the victim's skin. Grannie realized people would repeat the sad times of the past if no one is willing to take the stance needed in each generation. Grannie got her keys and headed downtown, as she arrived downtown, she saw so many young people upset and in tears over the events that took place, so much hatred filled the air. Grannie parked her car and walked around. She looked in the faces of many people, who were hurt by the shooting that took place.

As she looked in their faces, she went back to that memory of her and her grandmother on the sofa. Mattie, as you set forth in life, I need you to understand something, and Mattie said, "understand what?" "I see all I need to see, and it's unfair all that is taking place to my people!" Mattie's grandmother then said, "I hear you, and I do understand why you feel this way, but if you leave out what's most important in your stance then you miss the whole point of your calling." Mattie had no clue what she meant, and softly said, "I don't understand." Her grandma grabbed her hands, looked in her eyes and said,

"Mattie I'm talking about Justice."

God said, "we are to help those in need and be on the right side of justice;" that means for all people of all skin colors. God loves all people, not just one. You're trying to figure out how you can help your friends, looking for your stance and sweetie; I say stand, but stand in God, stand in His love for all people, stand for true justice, and if you do this, God will always stand for you. Not everything in life is fair and some things you may never understand, but I have learned in my life to lean not on my understanding, but in all that I do acknowledge Jesus and He has shown me the way." Mattie replied, "yes ma'am, but with all due respect grandma, you don't have to endure what black people endure. You don't have to enter a back room or be looked down on because of skin color."

Her grandma said, "listen to me and listen to me, good. You have a choice to make, and only you can make it, people have allowed justice to have two faces, one is hate, and the other is love. You can birth hate and feel that everyone different from you is against you and you hate them without knowing if that's true, not everyone is against skin color." "Hatred brings many things that are set up to destroy you, or you can birth love through justice and stand for righteousness, morals, honesty, fairness, and good behavior towards all people. When I married your grandpa, my family turned away from me because the man I married was black, we have seen and endured many things together, but what we've learned is that righteous justice is from God.

"Mattie if you stand for the right type of justice, you will never be color blind, you will never hate skin, and most importantly you will always remember that God made us all. He is fair, righteous and His behavior is different than what we hear and see around us. I'm not saying the road will be easy. I'm not saying that you won't be hurt or even hurt someone along the way, but what I am saying, is you must know what you are standing for.

If you allow hate to take over then who can you help?"

Mattie began to cry for she had never heard her grandma speak with such passion; she didn't realize all her grandmother endured to keep her family together.

Mattie gave her grandmother a big hug told her how much she loved her and went to meet her friends.

Mattie's friends asked, "are you going to Arkansas?" Mattie decided she was going to stand with her friends, but she would take her stance in her hometown of Kansas City, Kansas. Mattie watched as Ketta, Tawana, Kimberly, Debbie, Marianne, and Monique drove off to stand with those in Little Rock, Arkansas.

Just then Grannie snapped out of her daze when she heard someone calling her name. The young people were surprised to see Grannie downtown. They explained what the media left out. After that, they asked Grannie what they should do, and Grannie said, "let's sing!" As their faces quickly frown up. They all looked confused. "Sing," one young man said,

"Grannie, there's been a shooting, and you want us to sing?"

Grannie looked at him with this joy in her face and said, "music reaches the soul and changes the

mood." The young man started singing, and before they knew it, Ro Collins reported, "In Breaking News the sad events of the day have ended with many people coming together to pray for both families affected in the community today."

As Grannie drove home tears filled her eyes. She saw these types of events take place off and on over her lifetime. She thought to herself "it's sad how lives are still being lost due to skin color or pure hatred towards one another, but if people keep living and making a choice to overlook God, the breaking news reports will always sound the same. When will people realize their choices is where change starts." Then she remembered what her grandma told her about justice.

It was at twenty years old Mattie knew she would always stand for people and focus on what God says is right no matter the situation. Justice has no color and morals has a stance of its own.

You can read:

Acts 16:25, Colossians 3:12-16, Ephesians 5:8-19, Isaiah 1:16-17, John 3:16, Proverbs 3:5-6 and Psalms 106:3 to learn more.

I hope you enjoyed these stories, if after reading you have decided you would like to open your heart to God, all you have to say is "Jesus is Lord and believe in your heart that God raised him from the dead, you will be saved. For with the heart, one believes and is justified, and with the mouth, one confesses and is saved." (New King James, Rom. 10.9-11).

All we have to do is say sorry which means repent for all you have done wrong and do your best to live better from this point on. God will help you live right through His Son Jesus Christ, and His Holy Spirit, we are not left to do this walk alone, the living God truly cares for you!

If you have questions, feel free to reach out at:

yokedink.com

*Until next time,*

*Grannie*

God, what does Justice look Like?

# YOKEDink thanks you for your support!

We've added some bonus reads for you from *Grannie Knows Best- Breaking News* where you can read all 12 short stories.

Happy Reading and may God Bless you!

(A blessing is a gift from the living God which betters your life, understanding, heart, and situations. Many think a blessing only deals in things; God's blessings can cover anything concerning you).

# Bonus Stories

Intro- How the year started off..................................................

When Religions turn to one God...........................................……

Jesus is the Church!............................................................................

# Intro - How the year started off
§

GRANNIE was asked to attend a yearly community meeting at Lovell College two hours away. Many from the social world would be in attendance including Mayor Briggs, Senator Taylor, Fire Chief Miller, Chief of Police Robinson, Ro Collins from NJTT News and Get Down KCK radio Host J.D. Anderson; this is the first time Grannie has been asked to attend such an important meeting. Marlon and some other College students are part of the setup. Once Marlon heard of the meeting, he knew Grannie needed to be there. There was only one way Marlon could get Grannie on the list; he had to speak with Professor Knight, who taught Government.

Professor Knight is a person who loves titles, and for him, Grannie wouldn't make the list. Marlon knew what he was up against, but he also knew that he built a good relationship with Professor Knight over the last year. Marlon looked nervous walking into the classroom; as he entered the room, he began to speak very fast "Professor Knight, it's only right that a voice is heard from a spiritual viewpoint."

Professor Knight looked confused about the statement and asked him to repeat himself. Marlon took that moment to tell the Professor all about Grannie. Then Professor Knight replied, "Marlon, I'm not sure it's a good idea; she doesn't sound like a good fit. She sounds as if she lacks what's needed for this meeting."

After Professor Knight said, "Grannie lacks something," Marlon replied with madness in his voice, "what does she lack?"

Professor Knight stated, "Marlon talking about God doesn't qualify you for the big leagues!" Before Marlon spoke another word that he couldn't take back, he looked the Professor in his eyes, told him thank you and walked towards the door.

Once Marlon exited the building heading to his dorm, he said a few words in prayer and carried on with his day. Two weeks later Professor

Knight asked Marlon to meet him after class, once they completed last-minute details for the meeting. The Professor told Marlon to invite Grannie. Marlon looked up and said, "thanks, God."

As he walked to his next class, he called and invited Grannie to the meeting. Grannie asked Marlon "what do you look to accomplish by bringing me there?" Grannie wasn't clear why she was being asked to attend. Marlon replied, "Grannie there will be three topics addressed, and no spirit filled voice has been heard in years." Grannie became excited and said, "Marlon I would love to come." She wrote down all the information, said, "thank you" and ended the call. She then called June's dad her oldest son Christopher to inform him about the invite; Grannie shared the date, the time and asked if he would go with her.

Grannie was nervous.

She didn't know the topics up for discussion. She knew media coverage would be there, and that made her even more nervous. Grannie has spoken with people all her life, but not this large of a group; this would be different, for she understood words could be taken apart. At that moment, she did what she does best and started to pray.

"God, you placed me on Marlon's heart for a reason, and I thank you for thinking of me, move me out the way, and you have your way. Let your truth shine in Jesus' name Amen."

Later that night as Grannie got ready for bed thoughts crossed her mind, and she realized this meeting was the moment she and her husband often spoke of before he died. Mr. Givens and Grannie grew in faith together no matter how easy, hard, painful or uncomfortable a situation was they turned to God.

Her mind began to play back moments she shared with Malachi Givens. Malachi would say "Mattie one day all we've learned in life will be used in a way I can't even imagine." The thought made her smile as she got into bed and looked off into a daze. Before her husband passed away, he also told her "Don't worry, my love will always be with you, and you will finish what we started."

At that moment Grannie knew she was ready for the meeting no matter who showed up, God didn't give her a spirit of fear. Anyone God calls He justifies and glorifies them. Grannie said her prayers and rested for the night.

The phone call Grannie received from Marlon was just the start. The year brought her challenge after challenge, but through it all, she stood on her faith and let God's light shine beyond her tears. Get ready as you read how Grannie comes face-to-face with the realities of our world.

You can read:
Romans 8:28-30, 1 Peter 3:13-17 and
2 Timothy 1:7 to learn more.

# When Religions turn to one God
§

THE LAST FEW MONTHS have been busy for Grannie, her son Christopher reminded her to do something for herself. Grannie decided to listen and booked a history tour in a town near Nicodemus Kansas. During her drive to the tour, she started to think about something her husband would say. "Mattie this world would be better off if every Religion would join under the Living God. We were all made by the same God, yet we have fifty religions, but you know what Mattie? I believe many do know the way to live, some don't understand, and some just don't care, but you and I will always do our part."

Grannie smiled as she could picture his face, he was so passionate about others knowing the truth, he never forgot the wrong he did, he was determined to never be pushy but knew how important it was to show others how God changed him into a better man. Just then Grannie pulled into the parking lot for her two-hour tour. She was excited to learn the history of another city. Grannie made sure she had money to tip the tour guide as she headed to the meeting point. There was a tall young man with black sunglasses and a bright yellow shirt on which read "Tour today, personal history made tomorrow."

"Hello everyone and thanks for joining the tour, my name is Cedric, and I will be your guide just for today but what you learn will last a lifetime." "Are you ready to have fun? If I start sounding too much like your ninth-grade history teacher, let me know, and I'll try a different voice."

Everyone started to laugh for Cedric always used this open line to get the tourist comfortable.

After he gave the safety rules, he told everyone to follow him, and the tour began; Grannie enjoyed all that she had seen and learned, and Cedric made the walking time fun, they saw buildings from the 1800s and walked inside old houses full of history!

Then they came to a small church building, and Cedric said, "now this is the part of the tour where I get the most questions. This little church was built in the late 1800s and ran by the Quaker religion. Does anyone know anything about this religion?" A man lifted his hand and said, "I do, I know it very well, but please carry on." Cedric said, "that's what's up, maybe you can add some more facts to the story." As he went on speaking, he shared the story behind the family who belonged to the church.

"Now that you have that information let's get to the reason this building is last. One day a family showed up to these very Church steps needing help. No one was willing to help at first, so one day that same family walked in this building during Church service and said, what is a man called who is willing to help all people?" Everyone looked, but no one answered the man, so the man replied, "I'll answer this for you, what is a man called who is willing to help all people? That man would be called a child of God; for the living God gives us all the same treatment." As people of the church begun to whisper, the man stood in front of his family and kept speaking, "I came to this church with my family and was turned away, how can you call yourself men and women of God and yet turn those in need away?"

"The Bible you hold is the Bible I share with my children, and it tells me to try the spirit by the spirit, when you turned us away, I saw a spirit, not of the living God."

Just then Grannie looked around as all 20 tourists looked at this small church building and a lady name Sharon, she met was taking pictures.

Cedric said, "The words that black man said spread like wildfire throughout this tiny town and that night a Quaker, a Buddhist, a Muslim and a few other religions went to that man's house, knocked on his door and said, "can we speak with you?" The man's family was scared not knowing what would happen, for this was the late 1800's, and you all know the rest so let's move on with the story."

The man stepped outside, and the Quaker said, "you don't belong here, you came into my town and entered my church" just then the man thought to himself (my life is over, but at least I spoke up for what I believed in). Cedric looked around and said, "would anyone like to guess what happened next?" The tourist who spoke earlier said, "I would." Cedric said, "you have the floor please answer."

The tourist said, "what took place next is the reason I'm here today, the Quaker, the Buddhist, the Muslim, and the other men of different beliefs said to the black man. We have lived in this town in our different churches doing what God has commanded us not to do, we have turned to different doctrines."

"We all met up today for the first time under one roof and searched the Holy Bible after we read a few books we prayed together and asked the God of Heaven and Earth to show us who was right, and something none of us can explain took place in that building." The black man said, "may I ask what took place" with a look of confusion on his face for he thought he would die.

The Quaker stepped close to him "it was I that turned you away. I didn't expect for you to return, but you did, and because of you, we all understand that we have been wrong, we asked who was right and we all heard the same answer, we heard it very clear."

"I AM, Repent and search the scriptures and my truth will be reviled to each of you."

The men were shocked, but couldn't dismiss the encounter they all shared, and that night they made the choice to serve the living God together.

The tourist then said "can you picture the family's face as they heard these words. The black man realized that he wasn't going to die at least not that night! The town grew together and made history here, the Quaker taught the black man how to run a business, and he and his family opened a small cake and tea shop." Cedric looked clueless and said, "that's right but how do you know all this, have you been here before?" the tourist said, "no, but the Quaker you speak of is my great, great, great grandfather and the story is a vital part of my family's history."

"My family moved from here when I was a child, and I finally had to see it for myself. "Cedric said, "wow, now I have spoken to many tourists but never in a million years would I have thought of this moment!"

Grannie looked around once more at the faces and saw tears in the eyes of some, pictures being taken by many and others saying how amazing. Just then Cedric said, "I always leave this part of the tour for last, it's the longest and the most meaningful part of the tour for me. While I was in college studying history, I thought about joining a different religion, still to this day this little town believes in the same God and although this town is blessed, I wanted something different."

"I needed to see and find my way. I figured what's the big deal as long as I can say I have a god, but as soon as my mom heard about what I was getting into, she came to the college with a huge book. Inside this book was stories and news clippings, as I turned the pages it listed the name of the black man's family and I saw my great granddad's name Abraham West. My mother explained it all to me and then I learned the black man who came to this town was my great-great-great granddad, and his name was Elijah West."

Cedric went on to say, "can anyone guess what I did next" and everyone said, "no, what did you do?"

"I'm glad you asked" he said, "this group has the best questions" and everyone laughed! "I needed to know why I was just being told about this, my mom said there was a time she wanted to know the different types of gods, and she went looking. She also shared that once the world got done with her, she was calling on the living God to save her life and He did, which is how we ended up back here where I grew up at. After reading all the clippings my granddad kept from his dad, I understood many things and decided to come back home and start the tour company. I soon realized how much history was in my own backyard."

Cedric West thanked everyone and said, "that's the end of the tour, if anyone has any questions about food places or other sights to see just let me know." The tourist who spoke said "I came here just to see with my own eyes my history, I had no clue history would be made today, can we meet up to discuss our families?" Both men shook hands, and Cedric said, "Yes I know the perfect place, my mom's house she must meet you!"

Grannie thanked both young men for sharing such an amazing story, she gave her tip and said, "this is a story people need to hear, hidden history can have the biggest impact on a life, and this is good history. "As Grannie headed to her car she said, "God thank you for bringing those families together again, thank you for this tour and thank you for being the tour guide in my life."

You can read:
Romans 2:11-13 and Ecclesiastes 9 to learn more.

# Jesus is the Church!
§

GRANNIE DECIDED NOT to attend a new church this morning; she needed time to ask God what was next now that she has moved on from her former church. Grannie understands that she's living in a time where many don't care about the truth and when they do take time to listen, they fuss about it. Some people would rather hear words that make them feel good, but God spoke of this in 2 Timothy 4:3. Grannie's mom use to tell her "Church is in your heart" and it took Grannie years to understand that meaning, for when she was a child, she would ask how can a building made of bricks or wood be in your heart. Once Grannie moved from home, she began to realize what her mother meant. After Mattie and her husband gave their lives to God, she gained the full understanding.

Jesus is the Church, and when you give your life back to the living God and live for Him, the Holy Spirit lives in you and transforms your heart. All those years Mattie heard her mom say Church is in your heart, her mom was saying "God lives within you Mattie, and you can always go to Him no matter the time or day, Jesus is the head of the Church."

Now, this didn't stop Grannie from going to the Church building for she knew the Bible also says we should gather with others who follow Jesus.

It does our souls good to fellowship with like-minded people.

After all these thoughts crossed Grannie's mind, her phone rang, it was her son.

**Christopher:** Good morning mama how are you this morning?
**Grannie:** Hi sweetie, I'm good, and you? Where are Maxine and June?

**Christopher:** They're having a girl's day out, and I thought that maybe you would like to hang out with your favorite son.

**Grannie:** Now Christopher you know I love all my son's, no one is my favorite. I love different elements of each child's personality. I wasn't always excited about your actions, (Grannie let's out a big laugh) you boys knew how to push your dad's buttons.

**Christopher:** Yes ma'am, we did, but we also knew how fast to take our hands off those buttons. (Christopher laughs at the thought of those memories) Mama, I do miss him! He would be very proud of you, but also want to see you take it easy.

**Grannie:** I know Christopher, I know. What time should I be ready son?

(As Grannie got off the phone, she said)

"Lord; show me my next step. All these memories, and now listening to Christopher I know you're not done with me yet, but I must confess I'm getting a little tired. I'm watching people care less and less, but I know you'll show me the way; you always have in Jesus' name Amen."

Christopher knocked at the door, and he and Grannie headed on their way. Christopher pulled up in front of the park his parents took him and his brothers to as kids.

"I haven't seen this place in years," said Grannie, with excitement in her voice!

Christopher said, "once you said no church today, I knew you needed some time away from everything." Grannie smiled as tears filled her

eyes, she replied, "okay maybe this will make you my favorite son," and the two of them laughed. As soon as they sat down, Grannie noticed a small group of people sitting in the grass and said, "Christopher, what do you think they're doing over there?" He said, "I don't know mama, but we can walk by to see if you like." Grannie said, "no that's just too nosey," so they sat down and talked about old memories, just what Grannie needed. Then one of the men from the group name Cornell came over and said, "we see you've been here for a while; our time is about up but would you like to join us?"

Christopher said, "before I answer what are you meeting about?" The man stated, "a few of us have decided to meet up and have church service in the park when we can." Christopher and Grannie looked at each other, and then Grannie said, "who do you believe in?"
Cornell said, "with all due respect ma'am in my heart there's "ONLY, one Lord, one Faith, one Baptism and one God and Father of all!" I felt like I needed to come over and ask, but if you're not interested, I understand."

Just then the man started to walk away. Grannie yelled, "HOLD ON young man I didn't say we weren't interested we just needed to know who you're worshiping.
Nowadays people will call a trash can their Lord, anything goes in this world! We would love to join you." Christopher and Grannie joined the group and had a good time.

They sang a few songs and the man leading the group spoke about how spending time with Jesus can happen anywhere at any time.

Grannie expressed her excitement and said, "this was just beautiful, thank you for inviting us over and if you need anything or have any questions, please feel free to call us." Just then a young woman named Andrea and her friend Wanda asked," were you on the News when the community hosted the big meeting a few months ago?" Grannie said, "yes, I was." Andrea replied with a smile "thank you, ma'am, that was a needed discussion, and I hope to speak up for God like you did one day!"

Grannie told Andrea, "Well young lady this is a great start right here in the park, always remember Jesus is the Church which lives inside of you, and you can teach, preach and share His love with anyone willing to listen." Christopher shared one last thing, "remember where two or more are gathered in His name there God will be."

Grannie was thankful to God for a fantastic day and every situation He used her for and brought her through this year. No matter what Breaking News hits the air, God has an answer and is the answer for those willing to receive.

You can read:

Matthew 18:20, Ephesians 4:5-6, Colossians 1:18 to learn more.

Would you like to have all 24 short stories? Each book holds 12 stories, to read more about Grannie and learn how she shares that Jesus Christ wants to be a part of our everyday lives no matter the age or situation.

 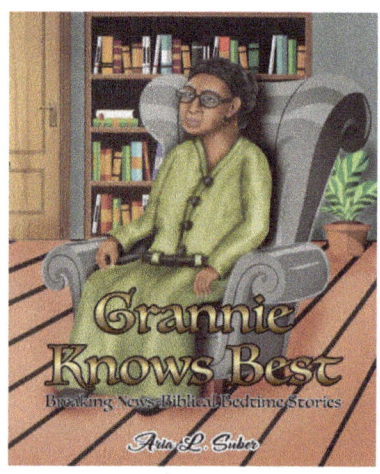

Grannie Knows Best Biblical Bedtime Stories

&

Grannie Knows Best Breaking News Stories

# Ten Short Stories pulled from Grannie Knows Best Biblical Bedtime & Breaking News.

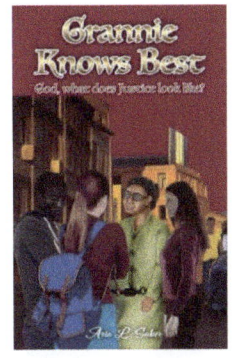

# Checkout the Stage play on YouTube or yokedink.com

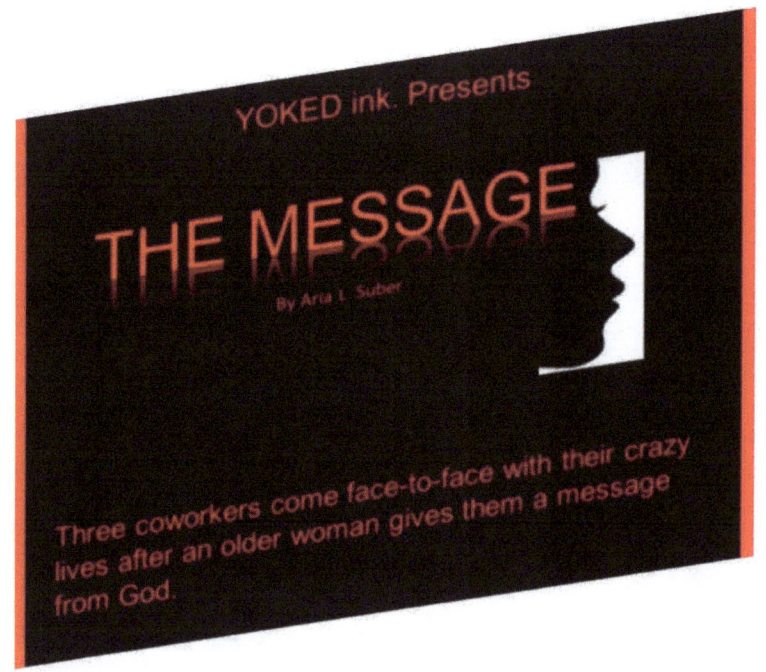

# Music: On most streaming sites.

# Keep Learning with YOKEDINK and check out the learning walls listed below at yokedink.com:

## Fruits of the Spirit
These fruits come only from the Holy Spirit, through Him we're able to perform/live out these fruits.

*https://yokedink.com/fruit-of-the-spirit*

## Acts of the Flesh
Our wrong desires can take us to places we never thought we would go, but the good news tells us we don't have to keep living in sin.

*https://yokedink.com/acts-of-the-flesh*

## What is Sin
Doing what the living God has told us not to do. Sin is meant to destroy our lives and keep us from the one true GOD.

*https://yokedink.com/what-is-sin*

**There's a full breakdown waiting for you, on the learning walls at yokedink.com**

# Reference

Nichols, contributed by: C. (2023, January 9). Little rock crisis, 1957 Retrieved March 10, 2023, from https://www.blackpast.org/african-american-history/little-rock-crisis-1957-2/

Publishers, T. N. (2011). Holy bible: New king James Version. Thomas Nelson.

Timeline: Key moments in black history. Black History & Civil Rights Movement Timeline. (n.d.). Retrieved March 10, 2023, from https://www.factmonster.com/timeline-key-moments-black-history

www.ingramcontent.com/pod-product-compliance
Lightning Source LLC
Chambersburg PA
CBHW040748020526
44118CB00041B/2806